W9-AVS-844

Outlearning the Wolves

Surviving and Thriving in a Learning Organization

by David Hutchens

illustrated by Bobby Gombert

second edition

PEGASUS COMMUNICATIONS, INC.

Waltham

Outlearning the Wolves: Surviving and Thriving in a Learning Organization
by David Hutchens; illustrated by Bobby Gombert
Copyright © 1998, 2000 by David Hutchens
Illustrations © 1998 Pegasus Communications, Inc.

Library of Congress Cataloging-in-Publication Data
Hutchens, David.
Outlearning the wolves: surviving and thriving in a learning organization /
by David Hutchens; illustrated by Bobby Gombert—2nd ed.
p.   cm.
ISBN 1-883823-50-1
1. Organizational learning—Problems, exercises, etc.   I. Title.
HD58.82.H88   1998
658.4'06—DC21   97-53299
CIP

Acquiring editor: Kellie Wardman O'Reilly
Project editor: Lauren Johnson
Production: Boynton Hue Studio and Nancy Daugherty

♻ Printed on recycled paper.
Printed in the United States of America.
First printing, March 1998.

Outlearning the Wolves
Volume Discount Schedule

1–4 copies $19.95 each	50–149 copies $13.97 each
5–19 copies $17.96 each	150–299 copies $11.97 each
20–49 copies $15.96 each	300⁺ copies $ 9.98 each

Prices and discounts are subject to change without notice.

Pegasus Communications, Inc. is dedicated to providing resources that help people
explore, understand, articulate, and address the challenges they face in managing
the complexities of a changing world. Since 1989, Pegasus has worked to build a
community of systems thinking and organizational development practitioners
through newsletters, books, audio and video tapes, and its annual
Systems Thinking in Action® Conference and other events.
For more information, contact us at:

Pegasus Communications, Inc.
One Moody Street
Waltham, MA 02453-5339
Phone: (800) 272-0945 / (781) 398-9700
Fax: (781) 894-7175
Email: customerservice@pegasuscom.com   info@pegasuscom.com

www.pegasuscom.com
5656

06   05   04   14   13   12   11

For Robbie

The First Chapter

This is a wolf.

This is a sheep.

Wolves eat sheep.

Any questions?

Wolves have always eaten sheep.
They always will eat sheep.
If you are a sheep, you accept this as a fact of life.

A flock of sheep once lived together in a beautiful, green pasture.

But the flock's existence was not a peaceful one. The wolves posed a constant threat, casting a shadow of fear over the pasture.

Sometimes, the flock would settle in to sleep at night and awake in the morning to find that one of them was gone—likely being served up to a wolf with asparagus tips and mint jelly.

There were several miles of sharp, barbed-wire
fence that surrounded the sheep's fields.

But the wolves came anyway.

It was hard to live amid such uncertainty.

Still, over the years, the flock got bigger and bigger and bigger. The occasional loss, though very sad, was to be expected.

This was the way
it had always been.

Another Chapter

This is Otto.

You should know that Otto will face an untimely demise by the end of this story.

Don't get too attached to him.

Otto was saddened by the rest of the flock's resignation to the wolves.

"I have a dream . . . " said Otto, perched on a hill where the rest of the flock could hear him. "I dream of a day when not another sheep will ever die to become breakfast for a wolf."

"That is absurd," said Shep the sheep. "You cannot stop the wolf. Remember the inspiring words of our ancestors: '*The wolf will come, just as the sun will rise.*' And also: '*Wolves. What jerks.*'"

"Indeed, I believe we are to be *commended*," said another sheep. "For we have prospered beneath the shadow of the wolf. Just look at how many of us there are!"

This made Otto even sadder.

"As long as the wolf is present, our strong numbers tell us only a half-truth," said Otto. "We tell ourselves we are strong so we won't have to face up to the ways we are weak."

Otto continued: "We all say the wolf cannot be stopped. But how do we *know* this is true?"

A sheep named Curly answered, "It *is* true. Why, even the fence that surrounds us cannot keep the wolves away. At first, it stopped them. But they must have learned to jump over it. Wolves learn very quickly," Curly added.

"Then *we* must learn—even more quickly!" said Otto. "We must make learning an ongoing part of life in the flock. We will become a *learning* flock."

"But we *do* learn," said Shep, mildly indignant. "Why, just the other day, I learned to pull a thorn out of my hoof with my teeth." (All the other sheep—especially those with thorns in their hooves—raised their woolly eyebrows in interest.)

"And I have learned to dig a hole. Watch this!" said Gigi, as she began vigorously clawing at the ground.

"Uh . . . I can push rocks around with my nose to make a pile," offered Jerome, who was just barely following the conversation.

An excited murmur arose among the sheep at these new insights, which, though perhaps obvious to you and me, were quite innovative and useful in the sheep world.

"This learning is a good start," said Otto, a little encouraged. "Ideas like these must be shared for the benefit of the flock."

"But to thrive in the shadow of the wolf, it is not enough. We need a different kind of learning if we are to be a true learning flock."

The flock looked down, sheepishly. They were trying hard to understand.

After some silence, Curly spoke. "Perhaps we could sleep in a circle."

Otto motioned for her to continue.

"Well," said Curly, "I think we could protect ourselves better if we slept in a huddle and not scattered all over the place. That way, when the wolves come, it will be harder for them to get us."

"But that doesn't really address the problem of the wolves . . . " said Marietta, a little lamb. But no one heard her. The sheep were too excited by Curly's idea.

"Yes, yes!" they all said. "Tonight we will huddle against the wolves. *Learning* may be a good idea after all!"

Otto was frustrated by the sheep's attempt at learning, which, to him, seemed awfully reactionary. But he felt relieved to see them at least united in purpose. This was a good first step. "The least I can do," he thought, "is stay awake tonight and keep guard while they sleep."

(WARNING! This brings us to the part of the story where Otto cashes in his chips. Take comfort in knowing that he is going to a better place where he will join Lassie, Old Yeller, and Bambi's mother.)

That night, Otto watched as the sky darkened and the sheep gathered together into a huddle. By the time the crescent moon was high in the summer sky, the flock had fallen fast asleep.

The next morning, Otto was gone.

Yet Another Chapter

When the flock woke the next morning to find Otto gone, they were devastated.

"Otto was a good sheep," sighed Shep.

"He showed us a vision of a better day," eulogized Curly.

"He had fleece as white as snow," someone said from the back.

Jerome didn't say anything. He just pushed a bunch of rocks into a pile with his nose—perhaps not the most effective coping mechanism, but it seemed to work for him.

But the mood soon turned sour.

"Those wolves! This is all their fault!" moaned Curly.

"What are we supposed to do?" cried Shep. "The wolves are smart, and they are strong, and they cannot be stopped. Our lives would be so much better if there were no wolves."

"If only that stupid fence were taller, so the wolves could not jump over it."

The flock sat there, dejected and miserable.

Finally, Marietta, the little lamb, spoke again.

"How come the wolves only come sometimes, and not all the time?" she asked the flock.

Everyone stopped. They looked confused.

Marietta continued. "If wolves are smart, and they can jump over the fence anytime they want, how come they don't come *every* night? If I were a wolf, that's what *I* would do. I would feast on sheep all the time."

The others looked even more confused.

"All I'm saying," said Marietta, "is that maybe the wolves aren't as unstoppable as we think. *Something* is stopping them, at least some of the time."

"What are you getting at, Marietta?" asked Shep.

"I'm saying the same thing Otto said. We must learn. We must do it together. And we must learn faster than the wolves."

"We tried being a learning flock already," said Shep. "And look where it got Otto."

"That's because we've only just started," said the wise little lamb. "Look at what just happened: We tried something *different,* but the results we got were the same. What does that tell you?"

Everyone had to admit that it was a pretty good question. But no one had an answer.

Marietta explained: "It tells *me* it isn't enough just to change the way we do things. We must also change the way we *see* and the way we *think.* We need to learn *how to learn differently.*"

"How?" everyone wanted to know.

"We can start by doing three things:

"One, remember Otto's vision: *Someday, not another sheep will ever die because of wolves.* If we keep that in mind, I think we'll know what to do.

"Two, let's take stock of what we believe. Everyone says that wolves are too smart, and cannot be stopped. We have made all of our decisions thinking that this is true, and maybe it is. *But what if it isn't?*

"Three, let's figure out how to do things differently. What do we have to do to stop the wolves? What is it like to *be* a wolf? Let's go out and get some ideas and information. Let's find out as much about the wolves as we can. Then, let's share everything we know with each other.

"Why don't we each do some thinking on our own, and then meet here this afternoon to talk?"

The meeting adjourned, and the sheep all went their separate ways, lost in thought.

Some of the sheep struggled with what Marietta had said:

"Learning may be all well and good. But if that fence isn't tall enough to keep out wolves, there is nothing we can do. We don't have the tools to make it taller."

"I won't stand for this kind of disrespect to our ancestors. They taught us that wolves were a fact of life. That little ewe is making a mockery of our heritage."

But some of the sheep took what Marietta said
to heart:

"Marietta is right. The
wolves only seem to
come at certain times.
That doesn't make
sense."

"Last summer, when we
had the drought, the
wolves seemed to come
much more often.
Hmmmm. . . . "

"Maybe the wolves *aren't*
jumping over the fence. It's
pretty high . . . and I don't
think any animal is *that*
strong. . . . "

Later that afternoon, all the sheep came back together to talk. A feeling of excitement buzzed among them. (Impressed by the turnout, Jerome made an attempt to count the sheep . . . but, strangely, he found himself becoming so sleepy that he had to stop.)

Shep began the meeting. "Friends, we are here today in memory of our friend Otto, and his vision to eliminate one hundred percent of deaths due to wolf attacks. Does anybody have anything to share?"

The sheep shared all their thoughts.

They engaged in a deep discussion about whether a wolf could really jump over the fence.

They discussed the strange timing of WRCs (Wolf-Related Casualties), and how they seemed to decrease after hard rains and increase during hot and dry periods.

They even confessed how difficult it was for them to rethink their own long-held beliefs about wolves.

Just talking about these things energized the flock and gave them hope.

Suddenly, Curly came trotting up, out of breath but very excited.

"Follow me! Hurry!" she said.

Confused, the sheep ran off after her, not at all sure where Curly was leading them.

The Final Chapter

The flock hurried after Curly for about a mile. Soon they came to the fence, right at the spot where a small stream ran underneath it. This was the same stream where the sheep often drank— although never this close to the fence, for fear of wolves.

"Look!" Curly said, pointing with her hoof to the spot where the fence crossed over the water. There, just above the surface of the water and caught on the barbed wire, was a small clump of sheep's wool.

"I was looking around for answers and I found this—but I don't know what it means," she said.

The sheep looked at each other in confusion.

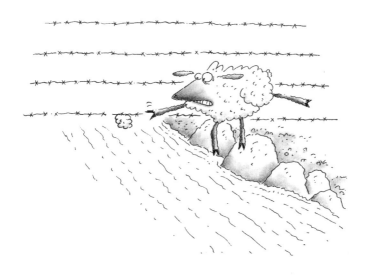

Finally, someone spoke up. "I got it! The wolves aren't going over the fence. They're going *under* it!"

Another sheep excitedly added, "*That* makes sense! When there is a drought, there is no water going under the fence. That's when the wolves crawl under!"

"And after it rains, there's too *much* water, and the wolves can't go under," exclaimed another.

The sheep got even more excited.

"So I guess that means . . . *wolves can't swim!*" Everyone laughed heartily at this.

Perhaps the wolves weren't so smart after all.

"There's only one problem," someone said. "We can't control when it rains. We're still at the mercy of the wolves. And now we're at the mercy of the weather, too."

The flock fell quiet.

Then Gigi spoke. "I think we're looking at the wrong problem again.

"It's true that we can't control the weather. But we *can* control the flow of the water. Watch this." And Gigi began to dig a hole, vigorously pawing at the ground under the fence with her hooves. Soon, some of the other sheep joined in.

"Don't just stand there! Everybody help!" someone called.

"Well . . . I can push rocks around with my nose to make a pile," Jerome offered, and began building a small dam with rocks, a few feet downstream.

Shep stood by, pulling thorns out of the hooves of other sheep as they dug.

Soon, a small pond began to form around the fence.

Amazed by this achievement, the sheep let out a spontaneous, collective bleating sound (an extremely irritating noise, but it sounds joyful if you're another sheep).

In the days that followed, the flock had a beautiful pond around which they could gather and drink and play.

But best of all, the wolves stopped coming . . .

. . . the sheep stopped disappearing . . .

. . . and the fear was gone.

"I'm glad we became a learning flock," the sheep would later say, as they nestled safely in to sleep at night.

"It feels good to know that we'll never have to go through anything like that ever again."

But maybe they would.

The End

Discussion Guide and Questions

What kind of a business book that wanted to communicate serious business theory would do so using cute, talking animals?!

Far too few! After all, having fun can be an important part of learning. And a metaphor, like the one in this book, is a powerful medium through which you can encounter new truths and new possibilities for the world *you* inhabit.

Behind their wisecracks, the sheep in this story have some important ideas to share. These ideas can have a far-reaching impact on the way organizations do business on a global scale, as well as the way you do your work on a day-to-day basis. Let's take a closer look at their experience, and see what lessons you can take home to your *own* flock.

Toward a Learning Culture

Much has been said and written about cultures of *organizational learning*. But what *is* a learning culture? How does one go about creating it? And what is meant by "learning"?

Every organization—whether it is a Fortune 100 firm, a sports team, the government, an elementary school, a church, or even your family—is faced with the challenge of *finding ways to create the results it desires*. Often, an organization must initiate both large and small changes to realize its vision. But change can be difficult. Indeed, in the U.S. publishing industry, the best selling category for nonfiction books is change management. Clearly, questions about these topics abound.

Change happens all the time. It's *easy* to create change. The hard part is creating change that is both *sustaining* and *transformational*. As Otto and Marietta discovered, this kind of change is initiated only when individual people (or sheep) are deeply engaged with

53

the change process, personally and emotionally. This is change that requires *learning*.

So let's return to our question of what learning actually is. *Learning* is continually enhancing one's capability to create, think, relate, and act in productive ways. Learning is innate. You—and your organization—are learning all the time, whether you intend to or not. The big question is, *What can we do to trigger this innate learning ability in ways that help us achieve the things that matter to us the most?*

This is the question Peter Senge addresses with his Learning Organization Framework (also known as the MIT Model.)[1] *Outlearning the Wolves* is built on this model; strip away the wolves, sheep, and story elements, and this is the skeleton you'll find underneath:

Domain of Change   Domain of Action

The framework suggests there are three domains that create organizational learning. The first, at the far right, is **Results**. This domain addresses the question "Why bother?" What are the measurable and observable outcomes the organization wishes to create? Otto articulated a highly motivating end result when he envisioned "a day when not another sheep will have to die to become breakfast for a wolf." He also said, "We will become a learning flock." Without compelling, clearly defined results, organizational learning does not take place. (It also won't happen if the intended results fail to tap into people's deepest aspirations.)

The Domain of Action is the next area. This is where much organizational theory is focused. It addresses the question "*What* will we do, or put in place, to achieve the results we desire?" Anything you can *plan, do,* or *see* is in the Domain of Action. People

1. Model is from Peter Senge, in *The Fifth Discipline Fieldbook* (Doubleday, 1994), pp. 15–47.

and groups who focus most of their energies here may find that they can indeed produce their desired results—but not for long. Over time, motivation and ability to sustain the changes will lag.

The Domain of Change is the final realm. Also called "The Deep Learning Cycle," this domain addresses the question "How will we pursue our goals in a way *that engages people's hearts and spirits?"* This is the mysterious and oft-ignored "people piece" of the framework. When we create environments where people choose to enroll themselves in the doing, we create the possibility for sustainable, transformational change. Note that you can't *make* someone engage in the deep learning cycle; people can only choose to enter into it themselves. That's why this model is so powerful, and so elusive. If a learning culture takes hold in an organization, it will be because of individuals like you who are committed to learning and growing.

So how did Otto, Marietta, and the rest of the flock create an environment where sheep chose to personally engage in improving their lives? Great question. Let's take a closer look at their experience of the Learning Organization Framework, and see what lessons it might hold for us.

————•————

Learning and the Domain of Action

Let's begin with the Domain of Action portion of the framework. Whether you are a flock of sheep or a global company, there are three areas in which collective, coordinated action may take place in order for a learning culture to germinate.

•**Guiding Ideas.** This is defined as *the best thinking people have to date about how to achieve the results they desire.* Guiding ideas include the beliefs, assumptions, and values that we hold about what it will take to create a particular desired result. Every organization

is governed by guiding ideas, whether these are openly stated or not. For example, a company may believe that only by hiring the top R&D engineering talent can it beat its competitors. In the story, the sheep were initially governed by a passive, unspoken guiding idea: We are victims, and merely to survive is success. Marietta broke significant ground when she introduced a radical new guiding idea: *that the flock could achieve the results they desired by first explicitly discussing their beliefs about wolves.* It was a courageous act, just as it is when anyone challenges deeply held convictions. (Remember the sheep who said, "She's making a mockery of our heritage"?) Marietta's new guiding idea catalyzed some powerful new behaviors in the flock.

• **Theory, Methods, and Tools.** These are the reusable, generalized areas of knowledge and practices people can draw upon, usually available in the public domain. They are especially important for testing *new* guiding ideas. In the story, Marietta called a

meeting, in which the sheep gathered around a rock to communicate. Nothing pioneering here; meetings, as a kind of tool, have been around for ages. But for the flock, the introduction of this method accelerated their journey toward their desired result.

• **Innovations in Infrastructure.** Many people think of "structure" as tiered boxes on an organizational chart. But structures are more than that. They are anything that directs resources (energy, time, money, attention, etc.) toward achieving the desired results. Of course, the sheep's pond was one new structure. In the story,

Marietta offered another structure in her speech to the flock: "Let's find out as much about the wolves as we can. Then let's share what we learn with one another." In other words, the sheep's new infrastructure involved an information-gathering and -sharing network. Sure, that's pretty basic. But it is an infrastructure nonetheless. In the sheep's case, this simple innovation produced some dramatic shared learning.

56

The Domain of Change: The Deep Learning Cycle

Organizations learn when people learn. And when people choose learning, they embark on a journey in which the destination is never reached. Yes, they adopt new ways of *doing* things. But more important, they embrace new ways of *being* and *seeing*. For people who engage in this kind of learning, a profound experience often occurs that might be described as an "awakening." Such people literally see the world and their place in it differently.

With this kind of perspective, the flock of sheep in the story ended up creating a pond that kept out the wolves and enhanced the sheep's quality of existence. It was an extraordinary collective achievement. The flock changed because the individual sheep were deeply engaged. Change takes place in three areas:

• **New Skills and Capabilities**. How do people know whether they are learning? Easy. According to Peter Senge, author of *The Fifth Discipline* and coauthor of *The Fifth Discipline Fieldbook* and *The Dance of Change* (three seminal texts on the principles of the learning culture), we know we are learning "when we can do things we couldn't do before." For example, the fact that Jerome learned to push rocks around with his nose was, in fact, legitimate learning. (At least, for him it was.) Transferring that skill into the new context of building a dam to create a pond that would protect the flock from wolves was an even higher level of skill building and learning for Jerome that benefited everyone.

Skills & Capabilities

Domain of Change

• **New Awareness and Sensibilities.** These are enhanced insights, or deeper understandings of the complexity around you that prompt you to question what appears obvious to others. For example, some of the sheep realized that "the wolves don't come after the rain, and they come more often when it is hot and dry."

Wasn't this obvious? Why didn't the sheep realize this sooner? Surely there were many opportunities over the years to observe this pattern. Maybe not. The reason the sheep missed this "obvious" pattern is that it *did not match their picture of reality.* It was only at Marietta's urging to challenge the belief ("We all say the wolves cannot be stopped ... *but what if it isn't true?"*) that the sheep were able to "see" and then explore this readily available information. It was a new awareness that the flock adopted with great struggle, but it produced a dramatic new future for them.

Skills & Capabilities

Awareness Sensibilitie

Domain of Change

- **New Attitudes and Beliefs**. New awarenesses ultimately lead to new beliefs. At the end of the story, the sheep had a collective realization: *Maybe the wolves aren't so smart after all. Maybe they really can be stopped.* Is it surprising that this new belief radically changed things for the flock? Think about it: The person who lives life believing he could die at any moment has a very different experience of life than the person who believes she is relatively safe from harm. The flock's *beliefs* about the world had a very powerful effect on the way the sheep *experienced* the world. When the way you view the world around you changes, *the world itself changes, too.* The flock's new belief about their world had immediate, tangible results. Their lifestyle ("confidence replaced their fearful existence ..."); their future ("wolves stopped coming ... sheep stopped disappearing ..."); and even the landscape of their pasture all changed. The story is a metaphor for the real power that is available to organizations in which individuals are constantly growing and learning.

Skills & Capabilities

Attitudes & Beliefs

Awareness & Sensibilities

Domain of Change

So Where Do I Begin?

In *The Fifth Discipline,* Peter Senge explores five disciplines at considerable length. These disciplines help organizations develop the *skills* and *capabilities* that kick the domain of change (the deep learning cycle) into gear. Briefly, the five disciplines are:

- **Systems Thinking**. Events in our lives are rarely as simple and direct as they appear. *Systems thinking* is the practical application of *system dynamics*—a field of study that examines the patterns and structures that govern nature, families, the economy, our bodies, companies, and all other dynamic systems. The flock's original cause-and-effect view of the world might be "Wolf gets hungry, wolf eats sheep." But the sheep discovered that a more complex system was in play, whereby variables such as the weather, the wolves' limitations, and the flock's own biases all intersected and influenced one another in complex cause-and-effect relationships. Broader systemic awareness gave the sheep the power to grasp some of these complexities and thus act in more productive ways.

- **Personal Mastery**. Personal mastery is the ability to create the results you want with an economy of means. People with a deep sense of personal mastery are on a life-long journey of self discovery. They are keenly aware of the results they wish to create ("I have a dream ..." said Otto [with due respect to Martin Luther King, Jr.]); their current reality (the flock's reactive posture); and the gap between those two states. People who practice the discipline of personal mastery may draw upon a deep, seemingly inexhaustible inner energy to create powerful results. Without a commitment to this discipline, we risk living in a *reactive* orientation, victims of the world around us. (Remember the sheep's complaint, "If only the stupid fence were taller ... !") For a closer look at this discipline, explore the Learning Fable titled *The Lemming Dilemma: Living with Purpose, Leading with Vision.*

•**Mental Models**. A mental model is a deeply held vision or set of beliefs and assumptions about how the world works. All of us have mental models; it is impossible *not* to have them. As we build mental models about ourselves and our world, these ways of seeing and thinking become more and more ingrained, until it becomes extremely difficult to perceive things in any other way. Ultimately, our experience of the world will begin to change to conform to our beliefs. Again, the flock's belief that the wolves were unstoppable is a powerful example of how mental models can affect the way we experience the world. Ironically, as long as the sheep *believed* the wolves to be unstoppable, they actually *were* unstoppable.

Mental models hold a great deal of power over us. However, in a learning culture, individuals can release the fierce need to defend and justify their mental models and become adept at challenging and "trying on" new ones. Exploring yours and others' is a great way to gain new insights and build a broader understanding of the complex world around you. For a closer look at this discipline, explore the Learning Fable titled *Shadows of the Neanderthal: Illuminating the Beliefs That Limit Our Organizations.*

•**Shared Vision**. Senge says, "When there is genuine vision (as opposed to the all-too-familiar 'vision statement') people excel and learn, not because they are told to, but because they want to." Building true shared vision has been the challenge of leadership over the ages. Too often, leaders generate *compliance* ("I'm just here to do my job … ") as opposed to true, committed *enrollment* ("I share the organization's goal, and I'll do anything to achieve it.") So how did Otto generate such strong commitment to his vision? A primary factor was that *the vision tapped into the sheep's own deepest aspirations*—in this case, the desire to live free of fear. That's a pretty compelling vision. You can see how it would generate very different results than a jargony "vision statement" to "increase quality, excellence, etc."

•**Team Learning**. True team learning occurs when individuals within a system are aligned in a free-flowing whole as they work together. Groups that have achieved this heightened state describe it in almost mystical terms. Sports teams may call it "being in the flow"; a jazz ensemble may speak of "hitting the groove," in which the music comes not "from you" but "through you." Perhaps you have had this experience in a work team in which all the members were deeply engaged in the task; you felt energized despite exhaustive work, and the output was far greater than you could have created by working individually. The phenomenon of an organization accomplishing something extraordinary (like sheep creating a pond) requires a deep, transformational *dialogue* in which team members can align in new, shared awareness about themselves and the world.

Questions for Reflection and Discussion

The above descriptions offer just a glimpse at the disciplines that may come together to enable the emergence of a learning culture. And now we're back to the original question: *So where do I begin?* Profound change can come from individual reflection as well as from conversations with others. Here are a few ideas to get you started exploring your own thoughts about the concepts in this book:

- *Draw from your own experience.* Think of a time when you felt completely aligned with a work team, your family, or some other group or community, when the energy was flowing, and the group achieved spectacular results. What was it about that experience that allowed this flow to occur?
- *Examine your own mental models.* What is your equivalent to "The wolves can't be stopped"?
- *Think about ideas.* Which ideas in this story and discussion guide do you find most compelling, and why?
- *Learn more.* Would you like to know more about the possibilities of the learning culture? Find out more about it. Peter Senge's *The Fifth Discipline* is a great place to start.

Often, exploring new understandings with others can powerfully enhance learnings that we gain through individual reflection. In that spirit, here are some questions designed to get you talking with your colleagues about the concepts in this book, and thinking about how to use them to make a difference in your own organization. Note: When we use the word *organization* in these questions, we mean your team, department, or entire company. Feel free to explore these questions together on any or all of those levels.

- How might the metaphor in *Outlearning the Wolves* apply to your own organization's ways of doing things?
- Has your organization stated the *results* it is trying to achieve? If so, how do the intended results tap into your own aspirations?
- Look again at the domain-of-action model (pp. 55–56). This model represents "organizational architecture," or those structures that shape how an organization does things. What are some guiding ideas at work in your own organization? How do these ideas influence the theories, methods, and tools used in the organization, and the infrastructures established? Now discuss some possible new guiding ideas to introduce into your organizational "architecture."
- Look at the domain-of-change model described on pp. 57–58. What does it mean to engage people in the deep learning cycle? How does your organization make it attractive for individuals to choose to enter into this cycle?
- How might the five disciplines help your organization develop new skills and capabilities within the learning cycle?

Remember, learning is a journey. It is not a skill or a technique; it is a discipline. It's a way of looking at the world. It is about growth and discovery.

The sheep came together to create a peaceful and prosperous existence, centered on a serene pond in a meadow.

What reality would *you* like to create?

Other Titles by Pegasus Communications

Learning Fables
The Lemming Dilemma: Living with Purpose, Leading with Vision
Shadows of the Neanderthal: Illuminating the Beliefs That Limit Our Organizations

The Pegasus Workbook Series
Systems Archetype Basics: From Story to Structure
Systems Thinking Basics: From Concepts to Causal Loops

The "Billibonk" Jungle Mysteries
Billibonk & the Thorn Patch   *Frankl's "Thorn Patch" Fieldbook*
Billibonk & the Big Itch   *Frankl's "Big Itch" Fieldbook*

Human Dynamics
Human Dynamics: A New Framework for Understanding People and Realizing the Potential in Our Organizations

The Pegasus Anthology Series
Reflections on Creating Learning Organizations
Managing the Rapids: Stories from the Forefront of the Learning Organization
The New Workplace: Transforming the Character and Culture of Our Organizations
Organizational Learning at Work: Embracing the Challenges of the New Workplace
Making It Happen: Stories from Inside the New Workplace

Newsletters
THE SYSTEMS THINKER®
LEVERAGE POINTS™ for a New Workplace, New World

The Innovations in Management Series
Concise, practical volumes on systems thinking and organizational learning tools, principles, and applications.

PEGASUS COMMUNICATIONS, INC. is dedicated to providing resources that help people explore, understand, articulate, and address the challenges they face in managing the complexities of a changing world. Since 1989, Pegasus has worked to build a community of organizational learning practitioners through newsletters, books, audio and video tapes, and its annual *Systems Thinking in Action*® Conference and other events. For more information, contact us at either address below:

One Moody Street
Waltham, MA 02453-5339 USA
Phone: (800) 272-0945 / (781) 398-9700
Fax: (781) 398-7175

www.pegasuscom.com